# The Anxiety Variety

by

## PAGE PARKER

# Table of Contents

# Part 1

# CHAPTER 1

## Mingle Mode

Like most people, I didn't realize that what I had experienced for most of my life was anxiety. As a child and throughout my teenage years, I never gave it much thought—I just assumed it was a normal way to feel. It wasn't until I got older that I fully understood how much anxiety had shaped my life.

I remember worrying about things as a kid, but I always figured they were typical concerns: the size of my thighs, calling to order a pizza, or trying to fit in with the cool kids in fourth grade. Pretty normal, right? I'm sure many people can relate.

I specifically remember my mom asking me to call Pizza Hut to place a to-go order. It horrified me. The thought of making that call made me incredibly nervous. What if I said something wrong? What would the person on the other end think? Would they be annoyed by a kid who couldn't get the order out clearly? What if they asked me a question I wasn't prepared for?

My mom would rehearse the conversation with me, making sure I knew exactly what to say and how to respond. She did her best to prepare me, but the anxiety still nearly paralyzed me. I'm glad she made me do it, though, because it's a life skill I use every day. Even so, the fear I felt in that moment was excruciating. My mom just couldn't understand why it was so difficult for me.

One of the most frustrating parts of anxiety is that people just don't get it. They don't understand the amount of anguish it can cause, even in the smallest tasks. What seems like no big deal to one person can feel like an impossible mountain to climb for someone with anxiety.

I still experience this in so many mundane situations. For example, I avoid phone conversations because they require so much effort on my part. I'm constantly worried that I'll say the wrong thing, mishear them, or not know what to say—leading to a long, awkward silence. And then comes the overanalyzing after the call. It's ridiculous! I spend so much time worrying about what I said.

This happens in person, too, not just over the phone. *Did I offend them when I said "XYZ?" Did I talk too much? I hope they didn't think _____.* You name it, I've worried about it. The only person I can truly talk to on the phone without fear of judgment or social awkwardness is my husband—he's vowed to love me no matter what!

My husband doesn't fully understand my level of anxiety over most of the things I worry about—mostly because he's the complete opposite. What causes me anxiety is either thrilling or trivial in his eyes. While he can't personally relate to how I feel in certain situations, he knows and anticipates my reactions and does his best to ease my discomfort.

That doesn't mean he just does everything for me to spare me from feeling anxious. I wouldn't even allow that because I believe in facing uncomfortable situations head-on. But the fact that he understands how I'm going to feel and lets me vent my anxiety out loud helps more than anything. Sometimes, that's all I need—to say it, get it off my chest, and move on. He knows this. He learned a long time ago that I don't need or want him to fix these things for me—I just need someone to unload them onto. He's my person for that, and I love him for it.

Making plans with friends is always difficult for me, especially when I know I'll be around people I don't know well. The thought of making conversation and keeping it natural and seamless completely drains me. I often have to force myself to go through with making plans. Once I set a date and time, I'll follow through because I don't like to go back on my word. But leading up to it, my anxiety takes over, and I start coming up with excuses to cancel.

Every time, I go through the same inner struggle—the back-and-forth dance in my own head. *I could tell them someone's sick. I could say I have to work.* I torment myself with these thoughts until I finally give up on canceling and decide to just suck it up and follow through. And of course, once I get there, everything is fine, and I have a good time.

It shouldn't be this hard to go have fun with your friends, right?

One of my good friends once invited me to join an all-girls book club. Most of the women in the group already knew each other from their kids' sports, work, or the gym. I only knew one person—a woman I had gone to high school with. She was a year or two younger than me, and though we didn't know each other well, she was always a sweetheart.

Before the first meeting, my friend said, *"You're gonna love these women. And I've told them how funny you are, so... be funny!"* Ugh... no pressure.

Oh man, the anxiety I felt before that first meeting nearly did me in. But once again, I sucked it up, pushed my excuses aside, and showed up. And my friend was right—these women were great. They were fun, funny, and real. The conversation flowed easily, covering everything from mom fails to husbands and kids.

Me? I stayed quiet. That's what I do when I don't feel comfortable or don't know people well. I stay silent for fear of saying something stupid or offending someone. And even though I barely spoke, I still berated myself afterward, picking apart everything I did or didn't say. I was *not* funny that night. Anxiety won. Hashtag... epic fail.

Funnily enough, in some social situations, I feel the need to make *everyone else* feel comfortable. When we're with a group of people who don't know each other well, I take it upon myself to keep the social wheels turning so everyone feels at ease and has fun. Isn't that a trip? I mean, *I'm* the one struggling internally with anxiety, yet I feel responsible for making sure everyone else has a good time. But if the interaction feels awkward, my anxiety skyrockets—so I try to be the social glue.

I definitely struggle in social situations where I don't know anyone well. Take the annual Christmas party for the Fire Department— my husband's job. I know these people. They're good people, and I love them. But every year, I stress about going because I know I'll have to socialize, mingle, come up with things to say, ask the right questions, and respond appropriately. *Ugh*. It makes me want to take a Xanax beforehand just to calm my nerves. (I wouldn't, but the thought definitely crosses my mind.)

I *hate* feeling that way. I look around the room, watching others, and I'm jealous—because I assume they *don't* feel this way. My husband certainly doesn't. He's comfortable in any social setting. He amazes me—always knowing the right thing to say, making people laugh, exuding confidence. I wish I could be like that.

Most of my friends, once they find out how much anxiety I have in these situations, tell me I have the best poker face. *"You always seem so relaxed and calm,"* they say. I'm glad I can fake it. But on the inside… I'm dying.

Part of my fear and anxiety in social situations comes from a lack of confidence—not just in my social skills but in my physical appearance as well. I constantly worry about being judged for how I look. I wish I didn't care what others think, but I do. I'm always concerned that I'm too overweight, that my thighs are too big, that my stomach pooch is unattractive, or that I look old. Even when I was younger, I obsessed over how my legs looked in shorts. No matter my age or body size—whether thin or plump—I've always worried about my appearance, and that alone has caused me anxiety.

I remember being a teenager and a young adult in my 20s, feeling so self-conscious about my body that I was hesitant to go skiing on the lake or attend a pool party. Ironically, I was probably in the best shape of my life back then and looked great in retrospect, but I still let my fear of judgment control my choices. When I did participate in those activities, I spent the entire time worrying about my appearance instead of enjoying myself with friends. Looking back, I just wish I had let it go and lived in the moment.

Going to the gym… well, it's just straight-up hell. *Are they thinking, "She shouldn't be wearing those leggings," or "She looks ridiculous doing that exercise?"* And if I see someone I know—an acquaintance—I struggle to find the confidence to say hello. I know… it sounds so stupid. And maybe it is, but that's how I feel. People probably think I'm a snob because of it, but really, it's just my anxiety getting in the way. Again!

If only they knew the internal dialogue running through my head, they'd probably be shocked.

*Oh, there's so-and-so. I should probably say hi. I'll wait until they look at me, and I'll smile. But I shouldn't stare—that'd be weird. Oh, they looked at me! I smiled, but I don't think they saw me. They didn't smile back. Maybe they don't recognize me? Or maybe they're just focused and don't want to be bothered during their workout. I'll just wait for them to say hi first so I don't interrupt.*

The random thoughts in my head are endless and usually end with me convincing myself that the person is upset with me, doesn't like me, or just doesn't care enough to say hi. I know it's completely ridiculous—and nine times out of ten, it's probably far from the truth. Meanwhile, that person likely just didn't see me or had something else on their mind. It's probably no big deal, but I let my anxiety blow the whole thing out of proportion until it feels absurd.

Overcoming the kind of anxiety that interferes with everyday life can be really challenging. So, what do I do about it? I just keep going. I force myself to make plans with friends, attend social gatherings, go to church, meet new people, and go to the gym.

As for phone conversations… I just text. It's easier, and these days, it's an acceptable form of communication. Except at work—there, I have to make phone calls to parents and other professionals.

Surprisingly, I've actually gotten pretty comfortable with business calls. Talking to parents, patients, or colleagues doesn't bother me anymore. It used to, but over the years, I've gained confidence in my job. That kind of comfort comes with age and experience, so I don't feel the same anxiety in those interactions. Thank goodness!

I just make myself do these things. I know in my head they're the right things to do—the things that will make me happy in the long run. I have to talk myself through the anxiety, push through the mental battles, and accept feeling uncomfortable for a little while.

In the end, I want these things for my life. I want relationships. I want to spend time with people. I want to do things, go places, and be part of society. So, I just do it. That's all I know to do.

# CHAPTER 2

## Workplace Worries

Workplace anxiety has reached a whole new level for me. Like most people, I spend half my life at work. I genuinely enjoy my job, and my chosen field of speech pathology is incredibly rewarding. But, like many professions, it comes with a great deal of stress and responsibility. Any high-level career that requires formal education and training is bound to be stressful, right? If it were easy, everyone would do it. Handling that stress is especially difficult for me. I have an intense desire to excel—I don't want to just get by or settle for mediocrity. My parents taught me that if you're going to do something, do it well. Give it 110%. No matter where I've worked, I've always given my all.

Over the past 20 years, I've worked in various settings. I started as an elementary school teacher, then transitioned to speech pathology, working in schools, hospitals, and rehab facilities. I've loved each setting for different reasons. But no matter where I am, one thing remains constant—I want to do a great job. Unfortunately, that drive to excel comes at a significant cost.

In my previous position, stress was just part of the job. There were legal issues to navigate, deadlines to meet, and many people to keep satisfied. As a supervisor, I was also responsible for keeping the team organized. My duties included coordinating educational opportunities, planning and organizing monthly meetings, and communicating changes or new processes and procedures. And the list went on.

In my current role, I'm once again a supervisor, but the responsibilities are far more manageable. However, I'm still the go-to person when other speech therapists have questions. I also review notes and evaluation documentation, provide feedback, and conduct peer observations.

One of the first things you learn as a supervisor is that you can't please everyone. No matter what, someone will always be frustrated that things aren't being done their way. As a people-pleaser who is deeply concerned with how others perceive me—as I mentioned in the previous chapter—this reality is especially difficult for me. I carry that weight with me every day.

Having a good relationship with my colleagues is very important to me. I strive to maintain personal and unique connections with each of them, making a real effort to show or tell them how much I appreciate them. However, there's always at least one person who resists that kind of relationship.

Over time, I've had to learn to accept that not everyone will like me or agree with me, and that's okay. When I'm not careful, though, work starts taking up too much space in my mind. Years ago, my husband pointed out that I was often grumpy or distant in the mornings before work—and he was right! I easily fall into the trap of overthinking. The moment I wake up, my mind jumps to all the stressors, problems, and tasks I need to handle, which immediately puts me in a bad or overly business-focused mood. This takes a toll on me and my family.

I've had to make a real effort to keep my mind off work until it's time. In the mornings, I focus on truly hearing my husband and kids when they talk to me, giving them the attention they deserve—because they are far more important than any job will ever be. The same goes for after work. I have to "turn it off," so I don't carry my stress and anxiety home. My commute helps with this; I have about a 25-minute drive, which I use to reflect on the day and mentally put it to rest before I get home. I also try to set a cutoff time for responding to work emails or texts.

I think I've gotten better at this over time. I've really had to teach myself to let things go, and I believe that skill comes with experience. Once I finally realized that, in the grand scheme of life, work stress doesn't really matter, I was able to stop letting it take up so much space in my head.

Work gives me a certain level of anxiety because I really want others to think I'm doing a good job. I worry about how my work is judged. Every time I plan a meeting agenda or write a report, I find myself wondering: *Is this detailed enough? Will they think this report is awful? Are they bored with this topic during the meeting?* The list of questions in my head never stops. My fear of negative judgment can feel overwhelming. Sometimes, I just wish I didn't care at all what people think! I envy those who act and speak freely without worrying about others' opinions.

Being in a supervisory role only amplifies this. If I'm responsible for other people's performance, my own work needs to be solid, too. I don't want to hold others to a standard that I don't meet myself. But this pressure can be overwhelming and leads to a lot of unnecessary worry.

That said, I do think I've gotten better at managing this stress and not letting anxiety take over. I'm learning to pick my battles, not sweat the small stuff, and let go of things that just aren't worth my energy.

Anytime you work with a large group of people, especially in public service jobs, conflict is inevitable. Conflict—ugh, I hate that word. Who actually likes conflict? No one, really. But it happens, and it has to be dealt with appropriately.

When I worked in a hospital setting, conflict was a daily occurrence. Whether it was with a patient, their family members, a physician, or other medical staff, it was never comfortable. I tend to avoid people I *know* I'm likely to clash with. There was one doctor in particular I dreaded interacting with because his moods were so erratic. You never knew if you were going to get a *"Great job, I appreciate what you do"* kind of attitude or a *"You don't know what the hell you're talking about—I'm the doctor, so do what I say"* kind of attitude. Whenever I had to deal with him, I would cringe. I literally had to give myself a pep talk and mentally prepare just to get through the interaction.

More often than not, conflict with him was unavoidable. When it happened, I could feel myself turning red—the heat creeping up my face from my neck. My ears would burn, my heart rate would spike, and I'd have to take deep breaths to keep myself in check. He made me *so* angry. And the worst part? This kind of interaction was inevitable every single time I had to deal with him. (I wasn't the only one—he had that reputation.)

Ugh. I hated that someone could make me feel that way, that his words and actions could trigger such a strong physical reaction. Every time I saw his name next to a patient's, I felt a wave of anxiety knowing I'd have to deal with him. Because of him—and other situations like this—working in the hospital was the first time in my life I had to seek help from my doctor and start medication for anxiety.

There's more to that story, but I'll get into that later...

These types of stressors and workplace anxiety are exactly why I have no desire to seek a higher position. More responsibility and greater demands only lead to more stress and anxiety. I know myself—I don't handle it well, and I doubt I'd ever be able to fully control my anxiety. Well, that's not entirely true. I *could* handle it, but I don't *want* to. I'm confident I'd do a great job, but at what cost? It's simply not worth sacrificing my mental health and well-being—not to mention the indirect effect it would have on my family. No thanks... I'll stay on the middle rung!

What has ultimately helped me manage my anxiety at work is self-awareness. Understanding my triggers and recognizing my mental limitations when it comes to handling stress has made a huge difference. I still struggle, but I've developed better coping mechanisms to ward off—or at least curb—severe anxiety attacks. Exercise, eating healthy, talking things out with my husband,

and managing my emotions through self-talk and prayer have all helped tremendously. Learning to control my reactions to people and stressful situations has also been a game changer.

We always tell our kids that the one thing they will *always* have control over is themselves—their reactions and responses to life. We may not have control over everything. In fact, we *never* have control over what other people do or say, but we *do* have control over how *we* respond. Lately, I've been working on applying that mindset at work. When someone complains or brings me a problem, I try to stay calm, consider all the factors, gather my thoughts, collect the necessary information, and then come up with a plan.

I've also learned that I don't have to carry the burden alone. Instead of taking full responsibility for every issue, I involve others in brainstorming solutions. When people help solve problems, they become invested in the outcome—and I don't have to shoulder the entire load myself.

These strategies have significantly reduced my worry and anxiety, allowing me to move on with my day. Overall, I've learned that anxiety isn't going away—but how I handle it is within my control. I can either let it consume me or push through it until I come out on the other side. I choose the latter—because the first option doesn't work very well.

# CHAPTER 3

## Paranoia Parade

I just want to have *fun!* I want to ride roller coasters at Disney World, go zip-lining in a rainforest, sing my heart out in front of a thousand people at karaoke, and snorkel in the Bahamas. There's just one tiny, *huge* problem... I might self-combust from anxiety before I ever get the chance. The fear of the unknown is *not* my friend. I'm so jealous of people who thrive on adrenaline (like my husband—he *lives* for it). They feed off the exhilaration of those experiences. Me? Pure torture.

When I was younger, I sang all the time. I was always involved in choir and show choir at school, and I sang at church nearly every week. I really enjoyed it, and I think I was pretty good for my age. I often entered talent shows and performed at special events like Christmas parties, weddings, and funerals. Sometimes, I sang in ensembles or duets, but I also did a ton of solos. I remember feeling nervous before performing, but never to the point where it held me back—not that I recall, anyway. I was confident, and my mom made sure I practiced constantly so I'd know my songs inside and out.

As I got older and went to college, I sang less and less. It was a natural shift—I wasn't part of musical groups anymore, my interests changed, and I moved on. Pretty normal, right? But every now and then, I'd still get asked to sing at church or the occasional wedding. Over time, though, my confidence faded. I'm sure that was because I was out of practice, but at some point, something changed. The idea of singing started to feel *debilitating.*

I still *wanted* to sing at church, and I would practice, but the anxiety I experienced was unlike anything I had felt before. It was awful. I tried *so* hard to push through it, convincing myself it was just nerves from being out of practice. But it didn't feel the same. The joy of singing had been replaced by dread. I started avoiding situations where I might be asked—or expected—to perform.

The church I grew up in was very small. Most weeks, only a handful of people attended—on a good day, maybe twenty or twenty-five, and most of them were my family members. I had been singing in front of these same people my entire life, so I *shouldn't* have cared or been so worried about it… but I was.

I started to hate singing. My mom and family couldn't understand what had changed or why I suddenly wanted nothing to do with it. Honestly, sometimes, I didn't understand it myself. Logically, I knew it shouldn't have been a big deal, but I just couldn't get past it. Knowing I had to sing that week would put me in the worst mood. As the weekend got closer, I became grumpy and irritable. By the morning of, I was an anxious, miserable mess. I just wanted to get it over with—I didn't want to do it anymore. There was nothing enjoyable about singing for me at that point.

Eventually, I started saying no to solos. I didn't mind singing with someone else or in a small group, but I refused to sing alone. I just couldn't do it anymore. The anxiety paralyzed me, and it got to the point where I dreaded going to church because of it. That wasn't what I wanted, so I simply stopped singing altogether.

This caused a lot of friction with my family. They couldn't understand how I had once loved singing and now wanted nothing to do with it. They just didn't get it, and I struggled to explain that it was all anxiety-based. If you've never experienced anxiety at that level, it's almost impossible to understand what it feels like.

That level of anxiety triggers a physical reaction—you become short of breath, shaky, sweaty, and completely consumed by miserable thoughts. Your heart races, and you do everything you can to talk yourself down from the proverbial ledge. It's an all-consuming feeling, making even the simplest task feel like an unbearable challenge.

On the outside, people probably assume it's just nerves. I even think I do a decent job of putting on a facade and hiding how I feel when I need to. But inside, the storm raging in my mind is *horrible*. It takes every ounce of self-talk and sheer determination to push through that kind of anxiety. The constant internal pep talk—the relentless effort to keep myself moving forward and just get through the moment—is exhausting.

If people truly understood what that feels like, they wouldn't push me to endure it.

About five years ago, we took a summertime vacation to Walt Disney World in Florida. The kids were beyond excited! Before the trip, I made a promise to myself—I wouldn't let fear and anxiety dictate my decisions and actions. I desperately wanted to experience the rides with my husband and kids, knowing this was likely a once-in-a-lifetime trip. I didn't want to waste it by being anxious. So, I was determined to push myself to be fun—for their sake.

The very first ride we went on was Space Mountain. If you've never been, it's an indoor roller coaster at Epcot, housed inside the giant ball that most people recognize. The ride takes place mostly in the dark, and the seating arrangement places each rider in an individual seat. My son, who was about six at the time, had never been on a roller coaster before. He can be a bit of a worrywart, too (yes, my genetics shining through), so we weren't sure how he'd handle his first roller coaster—especially one where he had to ride alone in the dark.

Oh my gosh… I nearly self-destructed on that ride. Not only was I nervous and fearful for myself, but I was also consumed with worry for my son. He was sitting in the compartment in front of me, and I couldn't see him, couldn't reach out to reassure him. It was dark, full of twists and turns and flashing lights—a personal nightmare for someone with anxiety.

At some point, after a flood of ridiculous, unrealistic thoughts—like, *What if he falls out and I don't even realize it because it's dark?* or *What if he passes out from fear?* or *What if he's crying uncontrollably?*—I finally had to accept that I couldn't control the situation. I just had to let go and wait until the ride ended.

And you know what happened? As we slid to a halt at the platform and the lights came on, I turned to check on him—only to see both of his hands in the air as he whooped and hollered. He was grinning ear to ear, screaming, "Let's do it again!"

Good grief. I was so relieved—yet so exhausted from the anxiety that I nearly fainted when I stepped off the ride. That day, I ended up going on two rides: one real roller coaster… and my own emotional one. A two-for-one deal!

The next ride I had to conquer was the Slinky Dog Dash. Don't laugh—I really had to work through my anxiety for that one. My kids knew it, too. They could see it all over my face and body language before we even got on.

We had to stand in a long, hot line for what felt like forever, and the brutal heat only added to my emotional "boiling over" point. The constant mental battle—talking myself out of being afraid, trying not to dwell on worst-case scenarios—was exhausting. That's usually how it goes: the longer I have to sit with my anxious, irrational thoughts, the worse they get.

My daughter offered to ride with me. She's just like my husband—completely fearless, or at least someone who enjoys the thrill of fear. She was amazing! The whole time, she kept me laughing and distracted, talking me through it until the ride was over. She was only about 11 years old at the time, but for those few minutes, she became the adult, guiding *me* through my fears. My little hero.

These kinds of irrational fears don't just take over my mind—they cause real physical symptoms. Shortness of breath, sweating, red blotches on my neck and chest, even shaking. Sounds fun, right? The mental warfare that comes with trying to stay calm is overwhelming. It *literally* wears me out.

I know that avoidance isn't the best way to deal with my anxiety. In reality, it only keeps me from doing things that might actually bring me joy. Other people seem to find joy in these experiences—why can't I? My husband swears that surfing is the most spiritual, peace-providing activity on earth. People say snorkeling in the tropics and seeing sea life up close are surreal. Zip-lining through the canopy of a tropical forest? Supposedly an unforgettable thrill.

But I wouldn't know—because I can't get past the fear I build up in my own head beforehand. And in my experience, when I *do* force myself to try something, I usually wind up enjoying it. (*Except for roller coasters. I still hate those.*) But the mental struggle leading up to it? Pure torture. So… I avoid.

I also avoid other things I'd really love to do—like having people over more often.

At our old house, we had a great space for entertaining with lots of outdoor space and a large swimming pool, but I didn't use it nearly as much as I should have. My anxiety about everything being *perfect* always got in the way. I've come to believe that caring too much about what others think and the fear of judgment are close cousins to anxiety. *Are they going to notice all the imperfections in my house? Do they think it's dirty or outdated? Are they silently judging our lawn, thinking, "Wow, they really should mow better around those trees"?*

I also avoid swimming in front of people because I hate how I look in a bathing suit. My legs are thick and covered in cellulite, and the thought of people seeing them—and judging me—absolutely terrifies me.

Once, a friend offered to give me a spray tan because she had just bought the equipment. Such a nice offer, right? But my immediate reaction was *hell no*—because that would mean stripping down in front of her, exposing all my body flaws. I joked that she'd be scarred for life!

Of course, she thought that was ridiculous. She reassured me that she wouldn't judge me, that we all have flaws, and that she didn't care. But no… I wasn't having it.

Recently, my husband and I were invited to a friend's house from church. It was a gathering of couples our age—no kids. I was really looking forward to it because I genuinely like and enjoy the people in the group. While there were a few couples I didn't know well (or at all), I still felt pretty comfortable about going.

When we arrived, several people we knew were already there, and we easily fell into the usual casual chit-chat. I initially stuck close to my husband and was naturally pulled into a conversation with the guys about real estate, investments, and similar topics. Not exactly my favorite subject, but I didn't mind listening and occasionally chiming in—it was a familiar and comfortable space for me.

Once everyone arrived, the hosts greeted us and explained how the dinner line would work. We all went through and then found seats at one of the tables. Since my husband and I were among the first through the line, we sat down before most of the group. A few people we weren't as familiar with sat near us—people whose names I knew but whom I hadn't really spoken to at length.

It turned out to be a great situation. The conversation felt natural and easy, and I wasn't anxious or nervous at all. They were warm, approachable people, which made my anxiety even less of an issue.

After dinner and a long stretch of visiting, the hosts announced that we'd be playing a game.

Oh no... *cue the anxiety.*

Immediately, I started dreading it. Playing a game I'm unfamiliar with in front of a group of people I don't know very well is one of my worst nightmares. The thought of not understanding the rules, looking stupid, or messing up in front of everyone was overwhelming. I tried my best to blend into the background, hoping they wouldn't notice me so I could just sit this one out.

No such luck.

"Page, you and Rich, come sit over here," someone called out.

*Ugh... why couldn't they just forget I was here and let me watch?*

Don't get me wrong—this group is made up of the sweetest, kindest people I've ever met. They weren't being inconsiderate; they just had no way of knowing how crippling this kind of situation is for me. From their perspective, it was just a fun, casual game. They were completely innocent in my anxiety.

So, once again, I had to force myself to find a seat and join in. Thankfully, a couple decided to move to another spot, which allowed Rich and me to sit toward the back of the group. That simple move helped tremendously—not having to be front and center took the edge off my nerves.

One of the women explained the objective and rules of the game to the whole group before we began. I'm sure her explanation was perfect. However, my brain just couldn't process it all. I was so afraid I wouldn't understand or wouldn't get the hang of it that I couldn't even absorb all the directions. I was too hyper-focused on the possibility of screwing up and being judged by everyone there.

Fortunately, once the game began, it went through about 20 people before reaching me, so I had plenty of time to watch and learn. When my turn finally came, I did a good job completing my task for our team. I'm almost certain that, from everyone else's perspective, I did just fine. They had no idea how much anxiety and fear that simple game caused me.

I spent the rest of the time hoping the next round would be the last. It felt like I was enduring the game rather than enjoying it like everyone else. Don't get me wrong—I did enjoy listening to and watching others play. There were plenty of funny moments and laughter from everyone. But ultimately, I was anxious about my turn with each round.

I bet all those people would be shocked to know what was going on inside my head the whole time. As I've been told before, I have a pretty good poker face in those situations. I think that's a learned behavior I've developed over my lifetime to cope. Sometimes, I'm better at it than others.

One of the things I've struggled with is throwing my kids' birthday parties. I always want to give them the best, most fun party with their friends, but the whole process overwhelms me. The thought of coordinating and communicating with others to make it happen makes me want to run away.

First, I have to reach out to all the parents and invite the kids. Then, at the party, I have to entertain the children while also making conversation with the parents. I'm so afraid of saying the wrong thing, and the pressure of socializing, keeping the conversation going, and interacting makes me nervous. I don't want anyone to feel awkward or left out, so I put a lot of pressure on myself to keep things running smoothly.

Knowing how stressful it will be—and how it will make me feel—sometimes makes me want to avoid having the party altogether. I secretly hope my kids will choose a family outing instead of a friends' party so I won't have to deal with the anxiety and stress. Of course, I would never say that to them. They don't know how I feel, and I wouldn't want them to because I don't want my anxiety to affect them. In the end, I push through my discomfort for their sake.

At the end of the day, I know I need to push myself through these situations. Maybe if I did, I'd gain confidence and realize it's not as bad as I fear—and maybe I could even enjoy it. If I keep trying to desensitize myself to the anxiety, maybe the mental battles would decrease over time.

Perhaps I just need to fight the fight. Avoiding it isn't getting me the outcome I want, is it? After all, isn't the definition of insanity doing the same thing over and over while expecting different results? Maybe it's time for a new tactic!

# CHAPTER 4

## The Great Escape Plan

Avoidance is a tactic I've used in situations both big and small. It can be anything from dodging a phone call to completely skipping a social gathering. While I know avoiding things that cause me anxiety isn't the best solution, sometimes it's the best option in the moment—just to buy myself a little time. Sometimes, I just need a moment to wrap my head around how to handle it.

For example, if someone calls me and I'm not totally comfortable talking to them, I won't answer. Instead, I'll text them or call them back later, but only after I've had time to gather my thoughts and mentally prepare for the conversation. I don't avoid it forever or pretend it didn't happen, but I will definitely procrastinate a little until I feel ready to tackle it. I like to run through the possibilities of what they might want to talk about, and from there, I try to think through my responses for each scenario.

Conflict is also a huge no-no for someone with anxiety. I mean, pretty much everyone wants to avoid conflict, but if you struggle with anxiety, you *really* want to stay away from it. This often means trying to control the narrative in certain situations—or just avoiding the situation altogether. There's that word again… avoidance. I can handle conflict much better when it's indirect. That's why social media, texting, or email are preferable for me. These methods give me time to collect my thoughts *and* collect my face.

I think I have a terrible poker face. My husband always says, "If people can't tell what you're thinking by looking at your face, they're idiots." Ha! Hilarious… but also bad. When I'm standing in front of someone, I don't have the luxury of reacting inappropriately—eye roll, cringe, gasp, frown, yell—then erasing and responding appropriately.

Avoiding people and certain situations all the time just isn't feasible. For example, you can't avoid family. I have certain family members who see things very differently than I do—politics, religion, etc. I always dread spending time with them because I worry these subjects will come up. I already know we don't agree, so I'd rather avoid them altogether. If I could start every gathering by saying, *"Okay, we're not going to discuss the election, church, or money today,"* I'd be happy. But that's not exactly socially acceptable, is it?

I get especially anxious when I know at least two people will be there who refuse to back down or avoid these topics. The moment one of these subjects comes up, things could turn ugly. Eeesh… shoot me. The thought alone makes me want to throw up. I don't want to be part of the conflict. I don't even want to witness it.

My husband thinks it's hilarious. He watches me trying to avoid eye contact, physically inching away from the people or situation, and desperately changing the subject—even if my transition is terrible.

*"So… how about the weather?"* He doesn't understand my anxiety about watching people argue or a conversation getting heated. To him, it's just entertainment. He feels no emotional investment in the exchange—he's just a bystander watching the show. To me? I'm cringing and experiencing second-hand conflict. I want to dig a hole and bury myself in it to get away from the drama. It sucks to be the self-appointed peacekeeper.

I'll even seem to agree with someone just to avoid conflict. I don't necessarily say I agree outright, but I'll smile and say, "Mm-hmm." Engaging by openly disagreeing just isn't always worth it to me. Sometimes, saying nothing is the best option.

Don't get me wrong—I can absolutely speak my mind and voice my disagreement if I feel strongly about something. Just ask my husband or my mom. But to avoid the anxiety that comes with conflict, I often just smile and nod, smile and nod. This is especially true when dealing with someone who has a strong personality, enjoys verbal sparring, and isn't likely to back down easily.

If I mentally prepare for conflict, I handle it pretty well. For instance, if I know I have to address an issue with someone at work, I can do it calmly and professionally. In some ways, this feels easier because the problem is affecting others, so it has to be dealt with. I still don't like it, but my anxiety doesn't take over in these situations—maybe because I feel more confident.

Work-related conflict also seems more manageable because it's usually about someone not meeting job expectations. Professional standards are clearly outlined, making the issue less about personal opinions and more about what needs to be done. It's not a matter of "my opinion versus theirs;" it's simply, "This is your job, and you're not doing it."

Additionally, handling conflict is part of my job, and I get paid to address these situations appropriately. Avoiding them isn't an option—I have to tackle them head-on.

At the end of the day, most people regularly avoid things they don't like or don't want to deal with. However, someone with high anxiety might rely on avoidance as a coping mechanism for a wide range of situations.

We might steer clear of a specific aisle at Walmart because we spotted an acquaintance and don't feel up to socializing. We might avoid using a new machine at the gym for fear of messing it up and being judged. Or we might skip a party because we don't know everyone there and worry they'll make us play a game.

In the long run, though, avoidance doesn't solve the problem—it's merely a coping strategy and not a very effective one. It doesn't bring about change or resolution to ease anxiety.

# CHAPTER 5

## Worry-Go-Round

Let's talk about emotions. Holy smokes—there are some heavy emotions tied to my anxiety: fear, sadness, depression, nervousness, anger, disgust—the list goes on. There are so many words to describe these feelings. Anxiety causes an overwhelming amount of overthinking and overanalyzing in my life. I have a talent for mentally beating something to death.

One of my strengths, in my opinion, is that I'm a relatively ob-servant person. I pay close attention to what's happening around me. I notice people's body language, facial expressions, and vocal changes to help me infer what they're probably thinking or feeling. It's a good quality to have because it allows me to anticipate their thoughts and actions—or simply relate to others better.

But on the flip side, I tend to overanalyze people's emotions. If someone gives me a certain look, it can crush all my hopes and dreams. I immediately assume they're mad at me or upset for some unknown reason. And just like that, the thought spiral begins. I start questioning everything I've said to that person over the last three years. Did I offend them? Did I say something that hurt their feelings? What if, when I said "A, B, and C," they thought I meant "X, Y, and Z?" Oh my goodness—I can really spin out of control with the overthinking.

But in reality, their expression usually has nothing to do with me. Most of the time, it's something they're dealing with or thinking about, completely unrelated to me. It just goes to show that letting anxiety control my thoughts and actions is a huge mistake. Anxiety always leads me down the wrong path.

This happened recently with a coworker. She and I are in supervisory positions together, and we're pretty good friends. We talk frequently through text and on the phone at work to discuss work issues and vent. I feel pretty comfortable with her.

The other day, we were supposed to be in a leadership meeting, but she wasn't there. So, I texted her to ask if she was coming. She responded with a simple "no" but then walked through the door immediately after. She gave me a strange look that I couldn't interpret—kind of a *What the hell?* look. I had no idea why she reacted that way, and it bothered me throughout the entire meeting.

I kept running through our recent conversations and my actions over the past week, wracking my brain to figure out if I had done or said something to offend her. As soon as the meeting ended, I had to leave quickly to make it to another meeting on time. But guess what? I couldn't let it go. The uncertainty of her response was eating me up.

Finally, I texted her and asked if she was mad or irritated with me. I think she was a little shocked that I even asked. She explained that when she replied "no" about coming to the meeting, she was just trying to be funny since she was literally walking in the door. As for the strange look? That had nothing to do with me—she was just wondering where our boss was since she usually runs the meeting.

You see? All that worrying and obsessing was for nothing. It had nothing to do with anything I had said or done, but I sure let it spur my anxiety!

Fear. Oh gracious, I think I could write a whole book on my own fears. Discussing the difference between fear and anxiety is kind of like debating the "chicken and egg" theory. Which came first? Do I have anxiety because of my fears, or do I have fears because of my anxiety?

I have fears about so many things—most of them completely irrational. Let me give you a little peek into my mind with my fear of zip-lining, for example. My biggest fear isn't falling (although that would definitely suck!); it's stopping.

I've been told that when you approach the end of the line and near the platform, you have to time it right and use your hand brake to slow down. But you don't want to slow down *too* much and stop short, or someone will have to come get you. At the same time, you don't want to come in too fast and crash into the platform—or worse, into someone else.

So, what's my fear? That I won't do it right. That I'll either stop too soon or not brake enough and slam into the platform. Either way, it probably wouldn't be the end of my life—or anyone else's—but I obsess over the unknown and how I'd handle the situation. I don't want to mess up and be embarrassed.

It's so stupid! Even though I *know* it's irrational, it still stops me from trying. I just *cannot* talk myself into it. And the most frustrating part? I *know* that once I do it, I'll love it. That just makes my hesitation feel even more absurd. Hmph!

We often watch TV as a family, and one of our favorite shows is *Dude Perfect*. If you haven't seen those guys and their antics, you're missing out. They take on all sorts of challenges and adventures, and it's always entertaining.

Recently, we watched an episode where one of them went hang-gliding in tandem. My daughter and husband, of course, were immediately like, *"I'd love to do that!"* My son didn't say much, so I'm not sure how he felt about it. But me? Watching the GoPro footage from his point of view had me thinking immediately, *No!* I could feel a knot of fear in my stomach just watching someone else do it on TV.

Before takeoff, the gliding instructor gave him a set of instructions: *Run and keep running until I tell you to tuck your knees up.* That's the part that would get me. I'd be so consumed with fear and anxiety over following the instructions correctly—so worried that I'd somehow mess it up and make us crash—that I wouldn't be thinking, *This is going to be amazing!* or *I can't wait to see what it feels like.* Instead, my mind would be stuck on every possible thing that could go wrong because of me.

I think my fear of failure and the unknown is crippling in some ways. I let fear overwhelm and paralyze me into inaction far too often. I know I've forced myself to push through certain situations in an effort to conquer my fears, but I don't win those battles very often. Honestly, I don't even try to win most of the time.

And it all comes back to that same question: Does my anxiety create the fear, or does the fear cause the anxiety? Either way, I know I'm missing out on so many things that I *wish* I could enjoy—things that others seem to experience so effortlessly.

That leads us to *regret*—the emotion that follows when I let my anxiety and fear take control.

A couple of years ago, we went to Puerto Vallarta, Mexico, with friends. While discussing excursions and activities, I mentioned the possibility of zip-lining. I really wanted to try it. There's a famous zip-line course there that stretches over the jungle where the movie *Predator* was filmed—about 12 miles of zip-lining. Everyone else had done it before, but they were all in.

But after overthinking it to death, I let my anxiety win. *What if I didn't do it right? What if I hated it but was stuck for 11 more miles? What if, what if, what if???*

And guess what? We didn't go zip-lining. The others were fine with that decision since they'd done it before. We went on other excursions and had an amazing time. But I *still* regret not doing it. I should have just pushed through my fear. Instead, I let my anxiety win, and I've been kicking myself for it ever since.

Regret follows me in so many other situations where I let anxiety take over—social interactions where I dwell on how I handled a conversation or moments when I failed to follow through on something I *should* have done. I often regret not being more confident and assertive with acquaintances. I wish I had the courage to take charge, to be the one who initiates a hug between old friends, to start the conversation. But too often, I let fear hold me back.

And I *hate* that. I just need to take the risk. I mean, most of the time, people will be receptive, right? They'll appreciate the effort, won't they? So why am I so afraid to make it? I truly regret those missed opportunities.

Allowing my anxiety to control me only makes me incredibly sad. I don't want to be consumed by fears and regrets. I don't want to overanalyze and overthink every little thing. But when I do, it leads to sadness—and ultimately, depression. Once I give anxiety the chance to win, I feel disgusted with myself. I loathe that I've succumbed to my fears. And once that feeling sets in, the mental butt-whooping begins. I beat myself up like it's my job.

This constant struggle and onslaught of regrets usually lead to some level of depression. I become so sad that I can't change the way I see things or the way I react. It's disappointing to know that anxiety wins most of the time. You always hear people say they struggle with anxiety and depression like they're a combo deal. And I think that's true. They are a combo deal—more of a cause-and-effect relationship than two separate illnesses.

Battling the emotions that come with anxiety is exhausting. Being aware of my emotions and understanding why I feel the way I do is an important part of the fight. I have to know my triggers and find ways to redirect my emotions when anxiety and worry take hold.

I have to stay alert and use strategies that help me cope. More importantly, those strategies have to be positive—exercising, eating well, getting enough sleep, staying busy, and having someone to vent to. I have to be careful not to rely on unhealthy coping mechanisms like overeating, oversleeping, or other destructive habits. I think that's why so many people with anxiety and depression turn to food, excessive sleep, or substance abuse—they're looking for a way to cope. And let's be honest, those negative coping mechanisms are often easier than the positive ones.

# CHAPTER 6

## Fear Pressure

I've always struggled with the fear of the unknown. I'm the kind of person who likes to be prepared and know everything there is to know about a new situation before stepping into it. If we were going somewhere new or I was about to experience something unfamiliar, I wanted to know exactly what to expect. Not having a clear idea of what was coming made my anxiety spike.

I see this in my son, too—he's the exact same way. My husband and daughter, on the other hand, are just the opposite. They go with the flow and adapt to whatever situation they're in. They don't worry about what might happen; in fact, I think they actually enjoy the element of surprise. That sounds excruciating to me.

I do think I've gotten better with this as I've gotten older, but it still affects me. We always laugh at my son because the moment we mention going somewhere or doing something new, he starts firing off questions: "Who's going to be there? How long will it last? What order will things happen in? What if this happens? What if that happens?" We work hard to help him cope and become more adaptable. We reassure him that if it's new for all of us, none of us know exactly what to expect—but that it'll be okay, and we'll figure it out together. And if we do have experience with something, we tell him every detail we can so he doesn't struggle as much with the fear of the unknown.

I think everyone deals with this to some degree. As adults, we may encounter situations like starting a new job, going back to school to further our education, or joining a new church. These experiences naturally bring a certain level of anxiety because we don't always know what to expect. However, as I mentioned before, I believe this improves with age because life experience builds confidence, and we become more assured in our ability to handle new situations.

For children and young adolescents, navigating new experiences can be particularly challenging. One of the biggest struggles for many young people is managing social interactions that arise in unfamiliar settings. In our family, we have always tried to pre-pare our kids for these moments. For example, if we know they will be around unfamiliar peers or adults, we practice and role-play potential conversations. We give them specific examples of things they might need to say or ask and then rehearse different scenarios. I pretend to be "Mrs. Unknown," approach my child, and introduce myself. My child then practices responding and using conversation starters. We also work on responding in a way that keeps the conversation going rather than shutting it down— something that seems increasingly rare among today's youth. We explicitly teach them to make eye contact, smile, and speak clear-ly and confidently so they can be understood. Learning how to engage with others socially can help reduce much of the anxiety that comes with new situations.

There's so much a person could potentially worry about regarding their future. We all have concerns about how we will manage or what will happen next. However, letting those worries control your actions, thoughts, and decisions can be overwhelming. I believe that understanding yourself—recognizing your fears and anxieties—is the first step to coping and managing them. You need to be aware of your triggers and have strategies in place to handle them effectively.

# CHAPTER 7

## Second-Guess Express

W hat's the result of all this anxiety? Well, let me tell you—there are many outcomes, and none of them are good. Over time, this ongoing battle can lead to depression, weight gain, lack of sleep, and a whole host of other physical and emotional symptoms.

I remember a few years ago when I worked in the acute rehab department at a hospital, I began to realize that anxiety and depression were taking a toll on me. That was the first time I truly understood what I was experiencing. In some ways, working in a medical environment was a blessing because it heightened my awareness of well-being and health.

I knew something was wrong when I started experiencing physical symptoms—elevated blood pressure, increased heart rate, shortness of breath, dizziness, and panic attacks. I just felt unwell overall. That job, while one I truly loved, was fairly stressful, and I wasn't handling it well. It was fast-paced, which I enjoyed, but it also required quick thinking, flexibility, and staying sharp at all times. On top of that, I was dealing with interpersonal issues with a coworker, which made everything even more stressful. And if you know me well, you know I tend to internalize things and carry them with me.

To make matters worse, it had been about three years since my father passed away, and by that point, everything was starting to come to a head.

My father was diagnosed with stage 4 lung cancer in September 2011. He fought hard but ultimately lost his battle in June 2012—the day after I had my son. I remember all too well getting the phone call from my brother while I was still in the hospital. He actually called my husband, and the moment I heard my husband's voice, I knew my dad had passed away.

Talk about overwhelming. It wasn't unexpected, but it was still devastating. It was a roller coaster of emotions—I was elated at the birth of my baby boy, yet at the same time, I had to process the loss of my father. Looking back, I don't think I was able to fully cope with both life-changing events the way I needed to. One had to be put on the back burner. Grieving my dad got pushed aside. I simply didn't have the time or emotional capacity to care for and love a newborn while also allowing myself to grieve properly. So, I didn't. Not the way I should have.

Three years later, I was working at the hospital and trying to keep up with life. My anxiety kicked into overdrive, and I began feeling awful. I was sad all the time. I had never lost all the baby weight and didn't feel good about myself. I avoided socializing. Then, one day, it hit me. I remember sitting in the car with my husband

and saying, "Something is wrong… I think I'm depressed. I think I need help."

Soon after, I saw my doctor, who prescribed an antidepressant. But I didn't stop there—I also made other changes. I switched to a low-carb, low-sugar diet and started exercising. Over time, I learned to manage my anxiety and depression better. I finally allowed myself to grieve my dad, and the physical symptoms faded.

The most important lesson I learned? Recognizing my triggers and taking action right away.

One of the most troublesome symptoms of anxiety, in my opinion, is lack of sleep. I don't think people fully realize just how essential sleep is to our bodies—we tend to take it for granted. Working in an environment where people were ill and struggling with sleep made me acutely aware of how much rest affects us, for better or worse. I've seen many patients completely lose touch with reality from sleep deprivation. They become agitated, irrational, and even furious. Sleep deprivation literally disrupts the chemical balance in our brains.

I now recognize that poor sleep has been a much bigger negative consequence of my anxiety than I used to give it credit for. It creates a vicious cycle that can quickly spiral out of control if left unaddressed. I would stay awake at night, overthinking everything I couldn't control, which led to lost sleep. Then, because I wasn't well-rested, my anxiety worsened the next day, making it even harder to cope with work and daily responsibilities. If I'm not careful, it snowballs on me.

Managing my weight has been a lifelong struggle. *Ugh*—I get so weary of this particular battle. Over time, I've had to become more aware of the *reason* behind my struggles. It's not just that I eat too much or indulge in junk food; it's that my eating is almost always tied to emotions. I'm definitely an emotional eater. If I'm sad, I eat. If I'm happy, I eat. I eat even more when I'm feeling down, depressed, bored, or just *blah*. Somehow, my brain convinces me that food will make me feel better. When I experience anxiety or emotional distress, I turn to food for comfort. Obviously, this makes it incredibly difficult to keep my weight in check, especially when anxiety gets the best of me.

The physical effects of anxiety can be both paralyzing and de-moralizing. For me, it's crucial to recognize my triggers—both for anxiety and depression—so I can manage them more effectively. This requires daily reflection and awareness. It also takes commit-ment to follow through with the actions and remedies I *know* work for me. Without that effort, I risk falling into the cycle of physical, emotional, and social turmoil that anxiety so often brings.

# CHAPTER 8

## Fraidy Cat Club

I had hoped not to pass my anxiety on to my children. I work hard to overcome it for their benefit because I absolutely don't want to teach them to be anxious. They are the number one reason I push myself through so many situations—I don't want to show them how to be fearful. I believe modeling, both directly and indirectly, is a huge part of parenting. Kids observe and watch every move you make, whether you realize it or not. They're like animals, feeding off your energy in every situation.

This is especially true of my son. He's much more of a "nervous Nelly" compared to my daughter. She eagerly tries new things and has no fear, while he requires much more encouragement and coaxing. If he perceives something as risky or dangerous, he won't want to do it. He has to be pushed and urged far more than most. That's why I have to be extremely cautious not to show my anxiety around him. I can't afford to let him see or feel it. Kids lean on their parents and trust them in all things—if he senses that I'm nervous about something, we'll never convince him to try it.

He's already showing signs of anxiety in his young life. Recently, during a trip to the beach, my husband had to have a "talk" with him because he was so fearful in the surf. Mind you, this wasn't his first time in the ocean—he's been many times and thoroughly enjoyed it. However, this time, the surf was particularly rough, with strong currents.

My husband and son were playing in the waves, body surfing, and having fun when my husband picked him up to take him a little farther out. That's when my son started freaking out. This really irritated my husband, and he got stern with him. He said, "Son, why don't you trust me? When have I ever put you in danger or done something to harm you?"

My husband was right. Logically, he has never done anything but protect our children. Most kids blindly trust their parents, no matter the situation. My son should know that, too—but this is where fear and anxiety take over.

Anxiety doesn't follow logic or rational thinking. In my son's mind, he can't reason through the situation and reassure himself that Daddy will protect him and everything will be okay. All he can think is, *This scares me, no matter what, and I don't want to do it.*

Ultimately, my husband convinced him to trust him, and they went farther into the surf, played, and had a great time. But it took comfort, reassurance, and convincing. I understand this fear and anxiety, but my husband does not. He just doesn't get it because he isn't plagued by the crippling anxiety we suffer from. I had to explain to him that our minds don't work like his—we struggle to rationalize in moments like that. I've learned to do it now, but it has taken years of experience, growth, and maturity to talk myself through those situations. We have to teach our son to do the same.

The fear of the unknown often triggers anxiety in many situations. This is true for me, and I know it's true for my son as well. In all things, I just want to be prepared for what to expect. It can be something small, like going to a new place, or something big, like starting a new job. My son is exactly the same way.

When he's unsure about what's going to happen, he wants to talk about it. He wants to know every possible detail so he can prepare himself and his mind for what's ahead. He seeks reassurance from me, my husband, his sister, and other family members. To some extent, I think this is normal—everyone wants to be prepared. But the difference lies in how we feel leading up to the moment.

Most people gather as much information as they can and then accept the unexpected as it comes. People with anxiety, however, will fold like a cheap lawn chair in the same situation. My son is definitely like this. If he isn't given all the details beforehand, he'll have a complete meltdown; although he's getting much better about this as he ages.

I completely understand this feeling, so I do my best to explain all possible scenarios in detail. For example, my son recently participated in a swimming competition, which was initially very overwhelming for him. He had competed before, but because of the COVID pandemic at the time, it had been a while—so it felt like his first time all over again.

As soon as we walked in, the environment was chaotic. My daughter took him by the hand and said they would go find out where they needed to be. She led him to one of the coaches, who told them to put their things down with the rest of the team and get in the pool for warm-ups. She followed the instructions, but my son, overwhelmed by everything happening around him, didn't get the reassurance he so desperately needed.

By the time I walked over to check on them—only about five to ten minutes later—he was already crying. One of the coaches was trying to talk to him and calm him down. I stepped in and asked what was going on. She said, "He's a little overwhelmed."

At that point, my son was near hysterics. When I asked him what was wrong, he said, *"I just don't know where to be, and I'm afraid I'm not going to be in the right place or doing the right thing."*

Ugh… I get it, son. I completely understand that feeling. His reaction is exactly what I feel on the inside—I just don't break down and cry about it (most of the time).

My daughter is able to roll with the punches and ask adults questions until she understands what to do and where to be. He, on the other hand, just loses his mind. So, I took him by the hand and sat him down. I explained that I would help him figure out where he needed to be and what races he would be in. I walked him through the process step by step, reassuring him multiple times that everything would be okay and that I wouldn't let him struggle on his own.

By that point, one of the other coaches, who was very sweet, offered to help him figure out what events, heats, and lanes he would be in for each race. She wrote them on his arm, and I explained how to read them several times. I answered all of his questions and went over the process until he felt confident in what to do. Then, I asked his sister to keep an eye on him and stay close so he would feel calm and have someone to lean on.

She's a sweetheart and even apologized for not getting him situated sooner. It wasn't her responsibility, but I thought it was so kind of her to care for him and understand his needs and anxiety at such a young age. Once he felt like he knew what was going on and what he needed to do, he was completely calm for the rest of the time. He even did very well in his races, taking first place in his heat in one of them.

I just have to take a moment to compliment my daughter further. She doesn't struggle with anxiety as much as my son and I—thank God! But she is incredibly in tune with my anxiety, and especially with her brother's. She truly seems to understand and anticipate his feelings.

The level of understanding she has and the compassion she shows toward him in those moments are remarkable to me. This isn't something we've explicitly taught her; she's just naturally observant of others' emotions and reads people very well. Her nature is to comfort and uplift those around her. She's like a little protective mama bear with my son. She would NEVER admit it—she likes to maintain the "big sister vs. annoying little brother" facade—but at the end of the day, she is always looking out for him.

I've had the chance to watch her interact with my son in social situations from afar. I've seen her notice his anxiousness and nerves, stepping in to assist and reassure him without him having to ask or say a word. She reads him like a book. What a remarkable talent for such a young human being—she's a gem!

I completely understand the internal struggle in moments like these. The feelings are indescribable. I want my son to know that everything will be okay, and I want him to learn how to navigate these situations on his own. He needs to understand that moments like this will always be a part of his life, and he has to learn to overcome his fears and anxiety by facing them head-on and problem-solving.

I've spent a lot of time enduring the mental warfare I inflict upon myself. I have to talk myself out of those feelings constantly. I fight this battle fiercely because I don't want my kids to develop the same patterns. Anxiety may be hereditary, but I feel it's my responsibility as a parent to equip my children with the tools to combat it. I don't want them to experience the same debilitation I do.

I recently interviewed my daughter about anxiety. She hasn't historically been an anxious person, but she's 17 now and in high school. I don't know if you remember, but high school can trigger anxiety even if you didn't have it before. It's a time of major hormonal changes, and teens are learning to navigate social issues, pressure, stress, and responsibility. I asked her about her perspective on anxiety—whether she thinks she struggles with it, what causes it, how she copes, and if her friends deal with it too. It was an eye-opening conversation. If you haven't asked your kids about it, you should. You're going to learn something about them.

She said she sometimes finds herself feeling anxious without knowing why. In fact, she told me, "I was anxious last night as I was lying in bed trying to go to sleep. I couldn't figure out why, and I was running through a list of things in my head, trying to narrow it down. I have my homework done, I don't have any events coming up that I'm nervous about, and I don't have any disagreements with friends or family… so I just couldn't figure out why I was so anxious."

I asked her how she knew she was anxious—specifically, what physical symptoms she experienced. She said she feels a nervous sensation and a pounding heart. Then, I wanted to know how she copes with that anxiety and what helps her find relief. She told me she usually tries to talk herself through it, reassuring herself that everything is okay. She also prays to God and asks Him for help.

Next, I asked if she has any friends who experience anxiety. She listed two friends she knows for sure struggle with it. She said she thinks one of them is on medication. I wanted to know what triggers this friend's anxiety and how it affects her. My daughter explained that the pressure of getting good grades and performing well in basketball causes her a lot of stress. This anxiety often presents itself through physical symptoms such as flushing, mild hives, shaky hands, and bouncing her knee out of nervous energy.

Her other friend also deals with a lot of anxiety. My daughter said, "Like, times ten!" I asked, "Well, what does she do that makes you think she's anxious?" She explained that her friend constantly worries about everything, repeatedly asking, "What if? What if?" She also shakes, slumps her body as if she's unsure and lacking confidence, and bites her nails.

My son overheard this conversation and said he imagines she's just like Anxiety from *Inside Out 2*. (Ha! Takes one to know one.)

# CHAPTER 9

## The Social Shuffle

Let's take a moment to address what I believe is a significant factor in our society that contributes to the development of anxiety and depression. I feel that our society has evolved into a remarkable and advanced state over the generations. As humans, we have learned so much and made countless advancements that simplify our lives, continuously pushing ourselves to improve. Our technological progress, educational systems, and societal infrastructure have expanded exponentially.

All of these advancements are incredible and have positively impacted our quality of life. However, I would also argue that these same positive developments have come with negative consequences.

Achieving greatness comes at a cost, regardless of the context. I believe men and women feel more pressure than ever to perform and excel. The social expectation for men to provide for their families, climb the corporate ladder, be actively involved fathers, share household responsibilities equally, and fully serve their community and church is exhausting, isn't it? The same applies to women. We are also held to an unspoken standard of being 120% productive at all times. We are expected to work full-time jobs, advance in our careers, have and raise children, serve as unpaid chauffeurs for our children's social activities, keep up with housework and laundry, stay fit and maintain our appearance, and actively participate in community and church activities.

I'm going to dive deeper into the woman's perspective here simply because I am a woman and feel this pressure so intensely. Personally, I feel expected not just to have a job but to build a well-respected career. I feel the pressure to advance professionally and dedicate the necessary time to do so. At the same time, I also feel the pressure to be a great mom. I mean… who doesn't, right? We all want to do everything we can to ensure our kids have the best we can possibly give.

I don't just want my children to have the essentials—clothes, toys, school supplies, and so on—I also want to give them every opportunity for new experiences that I can afford. I want them to participate in dance, gymnastics, theater, t-ball, soccer, tennis, swimming, and anything else they want to try. And with all of those activities come additional costs. We need to buy sports equipment, activity-specific clothing, pay participation fees, and travel across the country to make it all happen.

On top of that, I spend a significant amount of time each week coordinating logistics—ensuring they get to and from school, arranging transportation to their activities, and figuring out who will help with pick-ups and drop-offs since both my husband and I are at work. I coordinate with my family or whoever else is available to assist. I also have to make sure the kids have everything they need:

money, clean clothes for their activities, funds loaded into their lunch accounts, and so much more. The to-do list is endless.

All of this is essentially a full-time job in itself. I always say that when I get off work around 5 p.m. each day, my day is only half-way over. The same is true for my husband—it's not like I'm doing all of this alone. He's right there with me, sharing the responsibilities equally.

Then there's the expectation that we must always look our best and never age. We're supposed to go to the gym, stay in shape, be healthy, and look good at all times. Ugh. I fail miserably at this. Social media constantly bombards me with messages telling me to focus on my appearance. Ads and influencers are always pushing the latest diet, workout routine, skincare regimen, makeup to make me look younger, and teeth whiteners. You name it, they've got it. This is what our society values—perfection.

And what happens when people can't keep up? They experience negative thoughts and feelings, become anxious, feel defeated, and sink into the depths of depression.

I'm certain my daily and weekly experiences as a working, fully engaged member of society are no different from those of thousands of others. I think we all feel these same pressures. It's overwhelming. That brings me to my point—no wonder so many people are struggling with anxiety and depression. The standards set by society and our relentless drive for success have set us up for emotional failure. How could we not end up in the depths of depression? It's too much. It's impossible to sustain. We may achieve these successes, but we can't maintain that level of performance for long without suffering the emotional consequences. As men and women, we push ourselves until we experience crushing anxiety and depression.

We have to fix this. We can't keep pushing ourselves to the brink of mental illness just to meet unrealistic social norms. That's ludicrous! We have to find a way to "let ourselves off the hook," so to speak. We need to give ourselves—and each other—a break. We must stop being so judgmental and holding everyone to an unattainable standard that no one can reach or sustain.

# CHAPTER 10

## Viewpoint Voyage

One of the things I wanted to explore while writing this book was the perspective of those who know me—especially my husband. So, I asked him what he thought about my anxiety and how it affects me. Oh boy… talk about nerve-wracking. Nothing makes you feel more exposed and vulnerable than hearing someone's honest thoughts about your emotional struggles and how they influence your actions in life.

My husband's response was better than I had anticipated. He said he doesn't often notice my anxiety having a significant impact on me. He knows it affects me deeply because I tell him it does, but otherwise, he doesn't see me struggle with it outwardly. This was actually a huge relief to me because I had assumed he would notice it more than most. I think that speaks to my ability to cope over time.

He said the only times he sees my anxiety influencing my decisions are in certain social situations. Sometimes, when making plans for social engagements, I'll initially say, "No, I don't want to do that," but later, I'll change my mind. He believes I just need time to process it and talk myself into it.

He also said one of my greatest strengths is my ability to self-reflect and analyze myself in order to improve. I'm always striving to be a better version of myself in everything I do. According to him, I'm also a perfectionist, which explains my determination and stubbornness to make things happen—even when they make me very uncomfortable.

I recently had a friend ask me some questions about my anxiety and how it affects my life. She was very curious about my thoughts and feelings and why I experience them the way I do. I tried my best to answer, but I think it's incredibly difficult to put those emotions into words and help others truly understand them. It's hard for people to recognize those internal battles if they haven't experienced them themselves.

However, she also mentioned that I always seemed to handle things well and appear completely normal. She had never noticed any signs of anxiety and wouldn't have known about it if I hadn't shared my thoughts with her. Like I've said before, I think I have a well-developed poker face. Years of learning how to cope will do that, I guess.

Occasionally, I come across memes and posts about anxiety on social media. I'm always surprised by how many people I know—or am merely acquainted with—comment on how they feel the same. In some ways, it's comforting to know that others understand these feelings and constant struggles. In other ways, it saddens me that so many people battle this condition.

It makes me wonder: Have humans always struggled with anxiety, or is this a consequence of our evolving environment over time? This question led me to ask myself, *What is the definition of anxiety?* So, I did what we all do when we have a question—I turned to Google.

The AI-generated Google definition categorized anxiety as a noun: *"A feeling of worry, nervousness, or unease, typically about an imminent event or something with an uncertain outcome."* Below that, there were similar definitions, including one specifically under the subtitle of psychiatry: *"A mental condition characterized by excessive apprehensiveness about real or perceived threats, typically leading to avoidance behaviors and often to physical symptoms such as increased heart rate and muscle tension."* (Centered Chiropractic Website)

Until this moment, I had never looked up the official definition of anxiety. For me, this is confirmation—it perfectly describes everything I've discussed in the preceding chapters. Further research shows that anxiety is considered a normal response in situations like public speaking or test-taking. However, it becomes problematic and develops into a disorder when it is excessive, all-consuming, and interferes with daily life.

# CHAPTER 11

## Milestone Moans

One of the main reasons for increasing anxiety, I believe, is age. This is especially true for women, primarily due to menopause.

Now, if you're a man, don't skip this chapter just because you don't experience menopause. This topic is relevant to you, too. Every man likely has a mother, sister, spouse, or friend who has either gone through, is currently going through, or will eventually go through menopause. You would be well-served to understand the hormonal changes that occur during this stage of life. I would also argue that postpartum hormonal changes can trigger similar anxiety-related issues.

I can only speak from my own experience with anxiety during per-imenopause, menopause, and postmenopause. But reflecting on my journey, I feel compelled to share my story for the sake of other women. I wish someone had prepared me for this stage of life.

As I've mentioned in previous chapters, I've always dealt with a certain level of anxiety—even as a child, teen, and young adult. However, I noticed it most (and first needed medication for it) shortly after I turned 40. That's when I really started struggling. In Chapter Five, I talked about my symptoms while working in the hospital. At the time, I assumed my anxiety, shortness of breath, and high blood pressure were due to a stressful job, young children, and the general challenges of adulthood.

However, looking back—even since starting this book—I now believe my increased anxiety was actually the beginning of peri-menopause. I just didn't know it at the time!

Go ahead and Google the symptoms of perimenopause and menopause. You'll find a long list covering everything from cardio-vascular and gastrointestinal issues to menstrual and psychological symptoms—and it just keeps going.

Do you follow any women on social media, like Instagram or TikTok, who talk about these symptoms? You should. You'd be amazed at their stories and how similar their experiences are.

Here are the symptoms I've personally experienced: menstrual pain, irregular periods, weight gain, thinning hair, bloating, con-stipation, excessive PMS lasting most of the month, sore breasts, recurring ovarian cysts, brain fog, terrible memory, fatigue, joint pain, insomnia, irritation and mood swings, headaches, heart palpitations, hot flashes, night sweats, and—you guessed it—ANXIETY!

Just dealing with all those symptoms would be enough to cause anxiety, right? However, for me, anxiety was actually the first symptom to appear. At the time, I assumed it was just stress and job-related. The next symptom was ovarian cysts with pain.

Over the next couple of years, the pain would come and go until I ultimately had to undergo a unilateral oophorectomy (removal of my left ovary). My right ovary continued to develop cysts, but they were small and not painful, so my doctor opted to leave it alone. We didn't want to remove both ovaries at that point because doing so would have drastically reduced my hormone production—estrogen and progesterone—immediately triggering menopause.

Over the next 7–8 years, I continued to develop more symptoms related to perimenopause. Next came excessive PMS symptoms that lasted three out of the four weeks of most months. It was absolutely miserable! I experienced sore breasts, bloating that made me look six months pregnant, extreme fatigue, hair loss, and mood swings.

Up to this point in my life, I rarely went to the doctor—only when I was sick. However, I did have a primary care physician and an OB-GYN, both of whom were male. I loved and respected them, but when I started asking about my symptoms and concerns, I wasn't getting great answers. They listened and ran labs to check my thyroid function, but when the results came back within normal ranges for my age, their response was essentially, *Well, this is just part of life as a woman your age.* It felt like they were telling me to just deal with it—there was no help, no solution, only learning to cope.

I can't even begin to describe how defeating and frustrating that was. I remember asking my PCP about my hair, which was thinning and breaking off. I couldn't figure out what had changed or what I was doing differently. At the time, I had blonde hair that I paid for—I had been highlighting and bleaching it since my early teens—but suddenly, it started breaking off. My PCP's response was that I should probably stop bleaching it, as that was likely the cause. In my mind, I thought, *Yeah, but I've been doing this for nearly 25 years—what's suddenly changed?* But he wouldn't listen. He just wrote it off.

My OB-GYN was the same. He was a great doctor—until I had problems he couldn't explain. Neither of them seemed interested in investigating further. I wasn't satisfied with that. Reluctantly, I left both physicians to seek out another doctor who might actually help me.

I'm going into great detail in this chapter because if my story can help someone else recognize what's happening to them or a loved one, I want that for them.

After doing my research, I decided to establish a relationship with a new primary care doctor—a female physician. She was part of the same organization as my previous two doctors, which I specifically wanted at the time so she would have access to my prior medical records and complaints.

I remember that during my first visit, she asked, "Why on earth did you leave Dr. So-and-So?" (Everyone loved him, and he was well-respected.) I responded, "Because I think my issues are of a female variety, and Dr. So-and-So is a man who can't seem to hear my complaints or investigate them. I came to you because you're young, respected, and a woman. So don't let me down."

I was blunt, but I was tired of getting the runaround, and I wanted her to understand how serious I was about figuring out my problems. At that time, I still didn't fully realize I was going through perimenopause. She immediately started asking questions to investigate.

One question doctors always ask that I find so funny is, *"Are you fatigued or under a lot of stress?"* Well, those are relative, subjective concepts. I always thought, *Compared to what?* Yes, I'm fatigued and stressed—who isn't?

But let me clarify what I mean by *fatigue*. When you're experiencing severe fatigue, it's unlike anything you've ever felt before. I'm talking about the kind of exhaustion that completely shuts you down. It's not the tiredness everyone feels after a long day at work or from having the flu. This is debilitating fatigue. I would get off work and feel like I could barely make it home without falling asleep. Once I got home, I *had* to lie down and take a 20-minute power nap just to make it through the evening with my kids and husband. It felt like my body was shutting down whether I wanted it to or not. It was such an odd, alarming feeling.

I remember my new doctor running a bunch of lab tests to check my hormones, thyroid function, and more. And guess what? Those numbers came back *within the normal range*. Ugh—so frustrating! But here's what was different about her. She said—and I'll never forget these words—*"Your numbers look okay to me, but hormones and women's issues aren't really my specialty, so I might be missing something. I'm going to send you to a specialist."*

I thought, *Hallelujah—finally, a doctor who actually hears me and wants to help me investigate!*

At that time, she started me on a low-dose anxiety medication called Buspirone. I had tried Wellbutrin in the past with my previous PCP, but it caused more problems than it solved, so he took me off of it. I started the Buspirone, and within one week, I was already feeling better. The anxiety I had been struggling with was a direct result of perimenopause and fluctuating hormones.

I can't even begin to describe how much this helped. I had started to think I was just being dramatic, whiny, or making things up. I know the term these days is *gaslighting*, but that's exactly what I had been experiencing from my doctors and the people around me. It makes you feel like you're absolutely insane!

My new doctor then referred me to a female gynecologist who specializes in women's hormone health. I had an appointment with her within a week.

Now, I'll skip ahead and get to the point. This new doctor ran even more hormone labs, and when we reviewed them, she noted that while most of my numbers were within the normal range, some were at the very low end of that range. Based on those numbers—combined with my reported symptoms—she confirmed that I was firmly in perimenopause. All the symptoms I had been experiencing for the past 2–3 years, including anxiety, were a direct result of hormonal changes in my body. My testosterone was low, my estrogen was high, and those imbalances were causing my symptoms.

She said, *"I like to consider not only the lab results but also the symptoms you're reporting. If you feel like crap, then we need to treat those symptoms and see if that helps."*

Can I just tell you how relieved and mind-blown I felt at that moment? I mean, what a concept! I'm pretty sure I responded, *"That makes so much sense. Can you please explain that concept to other doctors?"*

Up until then, every doctor had focused solely on the numbers. None of them trusted the symptoms I was reporting. I guess they thought I was making them up or exaggerating what I was experiencing.

So here's what happened next: my gynecologist put me on oral progesterone and hormone replacement pellets.

If you're reading this and feeling skeptical about HRT, go do your research. My body was no longer producing these essential hormones, and I was suffering because of it. Once I started taking progesterone, it helped me sleep at night and regulated the estrogen in my body. That, in turn, reduced symptoms like excessive bloating, prolonged PMS, breast tenderness, and more. My periods became more regular, and I felt so much better.

The pellets, unfortunately, aren't covered by insurance. I have to pay for them out of pocket every 4–6 months, and they're pricey— about $350 a pop. But let me tell you, it's worth **every** penny. I would get a second job if I had to, just to afford them.

Since then, I've had a full hysterectomy (due to other issues), which immediately pushed me into postmenopause. I still rely on the pellets to provide my body with the hormones it needs. I can always tell when I'm at the end of their cycle because all those symptoms start creeping back—anxiety, insomnia, shortness of breath, heart palpitations, hot flashes, night sweats, brain fog, memory issues, and fatigue.

It's no way to live.

So… that was a very long story and explanation about how female hormones can affect you and cause anxiety. I honestly suspect this may be the case for men as well, since their testosterone levels drop as they age. Go Google it—I did, and guess what it says?

Mood changes, including depression, anxiety, and irritability. Sexual dysfunction. Decreased muscle mass, strength, and bone density. Increased body fat. Cognitive changes, such as difficulty concentrating, poor memory, and diminished cognitive function. Energy shifts, including fatigue, lethargy, and lower energy levels. And to top it all off—insomnia and sleep problems.

Here's what I really want you to know: You're not crazy! Your anxiety could be related to aging and a decrease in hormones that help regulate you physiologically. There is help. You don't have to suffer through it alone. Go get help, and don't let doctors make you feel like you're just a wimp who should suck it up. Find a doctor who will listen and actually help.

# Part 2

This part of the book is dedicated to offering solutions and recommendations, providing strategies to help you manage anxiety. This is not intended as specific medical advice or strictly evidence-based information. Rather, these are strategies that have helped me and others who have struggled with anxiety. My hope is that they might work for you, too.

I've separated each strategy into smaller chapters because I believe each one deserves careful consideration.

# CHAPTER 12

## Soul Service Provider (SSP)

I think one of the greatest solutions for my anxiety is prayer to God, reading His word, and my faith in Him. Sometimes, I wonder if my fear and anxiety result from not having enough faith in God. If I trusted Him as I should, would I really worry so much? Regardless, I do my best and try to trust Him daily.

One of the things I do every day is read the Bible. I truly believe this helps because fear and anxiety are addressed so frequently throughout God's word. When reading the Bible, it becomes so evident to me that God does not want us to worry. He says it over and over: "Do not fear," "Fear not," "Do not be afraid." These phrases appear so many times throughout the Bible. Some scholars report that similar phrases are used more than 100 times. God understands our anxious nature and how it affects us. He does not want that for us—He wants so much more. If only I could fully trust and listen.

When I'm feeling overwhelmed and caught in an anxious, panicked moment, I pray. God always listens, hears me, and helps. Every. Single. Time.

I believe God created prayer for us. He does not need a communication channel because He already knows everything—our thoughts, actions, and feelings. Prayer is for us. It is a way for humans to have a direct connection with Him. Through prayer, we can praise Him for His blessings and ask for His help. I suspect we all do the latter the most.

When I'm in despair, feeling overly anxious or nervous, my first response is to pray: "God, please help me navigate this situation. Help me say the right thing, do the right thing, and bring glory to You through my actions and words." I depend on Him to take away the feeling of panic.

I also believe God designed us to be great thinkers and problem-solvers. He has given us the ability to survive and thrive on this Earth, including the capacity to develop strategies that help us live good, productive lives.

# CHAPTER 13

## Treadmill Therapy & Mindful Munching

Other things that I have found helpful are diet and exercise. I know, I know… this seems to be the solution to so many problems—but it's true. The endorphins released during exercise genuinely help me feel better. In addition, when I'm exercising and eating right, I feel better about myself and gain more confidence. With increased confidence, I feel less anxious about most things and have a stronger sense that I can handle whatever comes my way.

I believe there's something to be said about eating the right foods to nourish both the body and brain. When your body receives the nutrients it needs, your hormones and chemicals stay well-balanced, helping to regulate emotions effectively. I also think sugar is the absolute work of the devil—it's intoxicating and addictive. In my experience, the more sugar I eat, the more I crave it. It's a vicious cycle that continues unless I put a stop to it. Sugar disrupts the body's balance and regulation on a biological level. When I let it creep back into my diet, I begin to suffer in every way: depression, increased anxiety, sluggishness, inflammation, and a general feeling of fatigue and malaise. Sugar is evil!

Exercise is an incredible tool that can solve many problems. For me, I've learned that getting on the treadmill or going outside for a walk or jog helps regulate my anxiety and the physical symptoms that come with it. Not only am I moving my body, regulating my heart rate, evening out my breathing, and sweating out toxins, but I'm also allowing my mind to purge negative thoughts. It's a release for me, and I think many people who exercise regularly see it the same way. It's a way to release the tension from the day—something about moving your muscles helps relax them. This is one of the best ways for me to manage an acute anxiety flare, and sometimes, I crave the release that exercise provides.

I have a close friend who feels the same way. She also struggles with anxiety and depends on daily exercise to help her cope with stress. It can be an effective anxiety remedy on its own. She and I both incorporate strength training and heavy weights into our workouts. I used to focus mostly on cardio, which is great, but as I get older, I want to prevent muscle loss and osteoporosis—and weight training is one of the best ways to do that. Along the way, I've also discovered that lifting heavy weights helps with my anxiety. There's something about pushing myself and practicing the slow, purposeful breathing required during resistance movements that makes me feel centered and regulated.

# CHAPTER 14

## Chill Pill Chronicles

Time outside in the sunshine is an essential element that helps me cope with rising anxiety. The natural vitamin D and increased serotonin from sun exposure are personally important to me. Getting outside—whether working in the yard, playing tennis, going for a walk, or just sitting by the pool—does wonders for improving my overall mood and outlook on life.

Talking to close friends and loved ones also helps. Sometimes, I just need to vent or say things out loud. I don't necessarily need the other person to give me advice or fix my problem—I just need to express it. My husband is a pro at listening. I trust him more than anyone else on this planet, especially when it comes to being patient with my illogical and irrational thoughts. He never makes me feel stupid for having them. Instead, he reassures me and encourages me to keep tackling my anxiety. I believe it's crucial to have at least one person in your life with whom you can share those thoughts and feelings.

The more you open up to others about your fears and anxiety, the more you realize how many people struggle with the same issues. I encourage anyone facing anxiety to find that person—even if it's a counselor or professional therapist. Talking about it and saying it aloud makes it feel far less ominous. Most of the time, when I share my thoughts and feelings with my husband, those issues seem much less troublesome.

Dealing with anxiety alone is such a lonely experience. It's like sitting in the dark with no hope. The longer you dwell on it, the bigger the problems seem. But once you open up, say it aloud, and share that darkness with someone you trust, it's like the clouds part and rays of hope start shining through. That despair begins to fade, and the problems feel more manageable.

I once read a quote that said, "Anxiety is highest during the 'witching hours' from late night through early morning. Be especially careful not to engage with your brain during these times." This is so true! The dark hours of the day tend to foster the darkest thoughts. It's important to keep yourself in the light.

I went to my doctor in November 2020 with several concerns. Long story short, she believed I needed help regulating my anxiety with medication. After discussing it and answering many of her questions, she concluded that I didn't necessarily need an anti-depressant along with anxiety medication. We both agreed that I wasn't struggling with depression itself but rather that moments of depression often stemmed from poorly managed anxiety.

After trying a couple of different medications, we found one that seemed to work for me. Over several months, we incrementally increased the dosage. My biggest concern with taking medication was that I didn't want to rely on it forever. I'm still fairly young in the grand scheme of things and don't want to be dependent on medication for the rest of my life. When I voiced this concern to my doctor, she reassured me that once I learned to manage my anxiety through diet, exercise, or other strategies, we could discuss the weaning process.

About a year after starting the medication, I felt I might be ready to taper off. Many of the initial issues I had discussed with my doctor turned out to be hormonal imbalances, which were successfully treated with other medications. Because of that, I thought I might be able to stop taking the anxiety medication. Additionally, by that point, I was on a higher dose, and the morning dose often made me dizzy and sleepy—something I hated.

My doctor supported my decision to wean off and provided me with a tapering schedule. I followed it, and within two to three weeks, I was completely off the medication. As I mentioned earlier, I've become pretty good at self-monitoring how I'm feeling.

About two months after stopping the medication, I started noticing some changes in myself. I was more worried about things in general and felt like I was constantly battling an overwhelming sense of doom—like something horrible was going to happen to me or a family member at any moment. I knew these thoughts and feelings were illogical, but I couldn't stop them.

I also became much more anxious about social interactions, something I hadn't struggled with as much while on the medication. When my husband's birthday came around, he wanted to celebrate at TopGolf with friends—something we had done for the past several years.

This year, however, felt different. I did NOT want to go. I dreaded it for at least two weeks leading up to the event. Of course, I never told my husband because I didn't want him to cancel—I wanted him to have fun and have something to look forward to. So, internally, I battled those thoughts every day.

Honestly, whenever something came up that might have forced us to cancel, I secretly hoped it would happen just so I wouldn't have to experience the anxiety leading up to the event. I just wanted that feeling to end. But I pushed through and made myself go.

On the day of the event, my stomach hurt so badly. I think my brain had convinced my body to be fearful, and it manifested as physical symptoms. Why did I feel this way? I can't even explain it rationally. I like my husband, I like our friends, and I've enjoyed TopGolf many times before. But I was so anxious about being social—saying the right things, keeping conversations going, making sure everyone was having a good time, etc.

On top of that, I had gained weight over the holidays and felt terrible about myself physically. I didn't feel attractive, I worried people would judge my appearance, and I just didn't want to endure that mental warfare. I wanted it all to end so I wouldn't have to go.

But you know what happened? We went—and I had a great time. It was so much fun, and I was so glad I made myself go.

But the struggle to get there? That was real.

That's when I truly realized I needed to go back on the medication. I hadn't struggled with these kinds of thoughts nearly as much when I was taking it. The very next day, I started back on my medication. Almost immediately, I began feeling better and handling everyday stress more effectively.

I hate that I can't seem to manage my anxiety on my own with just diet and exercise. But at the same time, why should I struggle and suffer when there's a solution that works for me?

# CHAPTER 15

## Hindsight Headquarters

In addition to the usual pressures of life that cause me anxiety, my doctor agreed that my anxiety was likely heightened at the time due to the pressing hardships and effects of the pandemic. I couldn't have agreed more. The pandemic had a major impact on all of us, affecting every aspect of my life—social, work, family dynamics, and more. So, for now, we medicate! And as mentioned earlier, we also discovered that I was in perimenopause, which was also contributing to my anxiety.

One of the things that has helped me most is my self-awareness regarding my anxiety struggles. Reflecting on how I respond to anxiety and fear has helped me change how I react. Over the years, I have learned not to be rash in my reactions to things that trigger my anxiety. I have also learned to control my emotions in the heat of the moment. Some of this probably comes with experience and maturity as I age, but I believe emotional control can also be learned and implemented at a younger age.

You have to be able to step back, gain perspective, and analyze yourself. You need to be in tune with the things that trigger your anxiety, which requires some tough introspection. You also have to be willing to ask those around you for their perspective on what they think causes your anxiety. I'm open to asking my kids and my husband what they believe triggers my anxiety and how I typically respond. It's hard to hear because no one wants to confront their flaws, but you can't fix a problem if you're not aware of it.

I asked my daughter to give me an example of a time when she noticed I was anxious and how I acted in those moments. She said, "Well, like when we're going on a trip and we're in the airport. You get very anxious about making sure we all get through security or get where we need to be. It comes across as you being angry and barking at us to be in the right place and take care of all our stuff." She added, "I know you're reacting that way because you're anxious, so I don't take it personally."

She's right! I get extremely anxious going through security. TSA agents are mean, and they will absolutely yell at you if your stuff isn't the way it should be. But wow, it really stings to hear that from your own kid, and I feel so guilty for acting that way. That said, I guarantee that the next time we're at the airport, I'll focus on using strategies to stay calmer and respond differently to my family in that situation. It's not just about hearing the feedback—it's about reflecting on it and making a plan to change how you handle anxiety the next time it arises.

In the past, if someone said or did something that upset me, my anxiety about the situation and how to resolve it would take over, causing me to respond in a way I later regretted. However, now, when something similar happens, I can talk myself through it and say, "It'll be okay. Just take some time to think before you respond." This helps me stay calm and collected, preventing me from creating a bigger problem than I'm trying to solve.

I've also learned to anticipate anxiety-inducing situations so I can plan ahead for how I'll navigate them. I think learning these tricks has really improved my poker face.

Finally, the thing I find myself doing pretty much all the time is talking nicely to myself. I know it may sound hokey, but positive self-talk is so important. I'm a firm believer that your brain will believe whatever it's told. If you constantly tell yourself that something will be bad, then it will be. Conversely, if you continuously feed yourself positive and encouraging thoughts, you'll believe those just as easily.

I find myself saying things like, "It's okay." "It'll be alright." "You can do this." "You're smart enough to do this." "No one will care." Your brain needs to be fed, just like the rest of your body. It requires food for thought. Reading encouraging works like the Bible or self-help books can really nourish your mental health. Listening to podcasts or music that uplifts you is also helpful.

I tend to only watch movies or TV shows that make me happy. The same goes for the books I read for pleasure. I stay away from horror movies, scary shows, or books with dark themes. I know a lot of people love those kinds of movies and books, and I don't judge anyone for enjoying them, but I just can't do it. They make me feel more anxious and uneasy, so I avoid them because I know I can't handle it.

# CHAPTER 16

## Strategic Zen

I recently decided to set some goals for myself this year. I didn't just want to outline my goals—I needed a way to remind myself of them daily. So, I made a vision board. I wrote down my goals, then started choosing pictures, printed them out, and glued them to a board. Under each picture, I typed out the goal. Once my board was finished, I hung it in my closet, in a spot where I'll see it every day—probably several times a day.

I've set goals for myself in the past, but I usually just write them down in a notebook or something, then forget to look at them. I put them away, and then it's out of sight, out of mind. And guess what? I don't follow through. I'm a very visual learner, and this year, I decided I needed something right in my face all the time to keep me on track.

Why am I telling you this? Well, because I think setting goals and structuring your time helps curb anxiety.

Having goals I want to reach by the end of the year has made me focus each day on how I can achieve them. I dedicate time every day to working toward these goals. For example, some of my goals include finishing this book, reading 24 books this year, reading a Bible chapter daily, working out daily, and building our blog and website. To accomplish them, I have to set aside time each day to make progress.

As a result, I spend far less time on mindless activities like watching TV or scrolling through TikTok. Now, don't get me wrong—I still do those things, but only after I've completed everything else. I swear it has helped reduce my anxiety because I feel productive, busy, and accomplished.

I also feel like being organized and eliminating chaos helps reduce my anxiety. Every morning, I make the bed. I didn't grow up doing this—my mom never required us to make our beds daily, only when we were expecting company.

Later in life, after I got married, I started making the bed every day when we listed our first house for sale. We had to keep it neat and clean in case potential buyers came for a showing. Over time, I realized I liked how it made me feel about my day, so I kept the habit. Now, more than 20 years later, I still do it every single day.

I also keep a very clean and organized house. My kids and husband give me a hard time and joke that I'm OCD, but I don't care. And honestly, I know they secretly appreciate it because they've all become more organized, too. My kids keep their rooms relatively clean and make their beds every day. Life feels so much less chaotic when your environment is neat and orderly.

Keeping the things around you clean and organized can help reduce anxiety—it's just nice to come home to a tidy space without that looming feeling of needing to clean up.

Coping with anxiety is a full-time effort. It requires constant self-reflection, an awareness of your triggers, and daily strategies for managing them. These strategies need to be positive and provide a path forward for change.

The brain chemicals associated with anxiety are norepinephrine, serotonin, and dopamine (although dopamine plays an indirect role and isn't the primary neurotransmitter). Anxiety is typically the result of an imbalance and complex interaction of these neurotransmitters. Fortunately, they can be influenced through strategies such as exercise, diet choices, stress reduction, relaxation techniques, good sleep hygiene, medication, counseling, and connecting with others who struggle with anxiety.

Ultimately, I face the challenge of tackling my anxiety every day. It's a constant battle, but one I can fight with the help of strategies, medication, the people who love me, and my Creator. My hope is that by sharing my story and perspective, I can help someone else. At the very least, I want others to know they are not alone.

If you struggle with anxiety, get help. Reach out—talk to your doctor, your family, your friends—and start implementing strategies. Don't let anxiety rule your life. No matter what kind of anxiety you face, you are not alone. I know how you feel, and there is hope. Let's conquer it together.

# Acknowledgments

I would like to give my deepest expression of gratitude and love to my husband for always supporting me. He encouraged me to write this book and has shown overwhelming support through each step of this process. He gives me confidence when I am lacking, he gives me faith when I have none, and he tells me how proud he is of me.

I also want to thank my children. They don't understand it yet because they are young, but they are a source of great strength and motivation to me. They are kind, loving, and genuinely want the best for me. Being their mom and watching them develop has inspired me to reflect on myself and how I can always improve.

Thank you, Rich, Hannah, and Cole, for always encouraging and loving me.

www.ingramcontent.com/pod-product-compliance
Lightning Source LLC
Chambersburg PA
CBHW061706120626
46550CB00003B/1117